24 EASY CLASSICAL
SOLOS FOR BASS

BOOK 1

HARRY HUNT, JR., MFA

ENTERTAINMENT, INC.

24 Easy Classical Solos for Bass: Book 1
Harry Hunt, Jr., MFA

Published by A2G Entertainment Inc.
Chicago, IL
harryhuntjr.com

ISBN: 978-1-954127-30-2 (Paperback)

Printed in the USA
Second Edition

CONTENTS

PLAY-ALONG & DEMONSTRATION TRACKS

To Stream or Download
Click or Visit
harryhuntjr.net/book-ecs-bass-bk1

OTHER LINKS

https://sites.google.com/view/book-tracks/bass

.

(bookmark the links in your browser for quicker access)

1. HOT CROSS BUNS

(Two-bar piano intro)

2. LIGHTLY ROW

(Two-bar piano intro)

3. LULLABY

Brahms

(Two-bar piano intro - pickup starts on beat 3)

4. AU CLAIR DE LA LUNE

(Two-bar piano intro)

5. TWINKLE

(Two-bar piano intro)

6. SCARBOROUGH FAIR

(Two-bar piano intro)

7. OH SUSANNA

Foster

(Two-bar piano intro - pickup starts on beat four)

8. MARRIAGE OF FIGARO

(Two-bar piano intro)

Mozart

9. LONG LONG AGO

(Two-bar piano intro)

Bayly

10. RONDEAU

Mouret

(Two-bar piano intro - pickup starts on beat four)

11. PIANO CONCERTO #3

Beethoven

(Two-bar piano intro)

12. SYMPHONY #7 (2nd Movement)

Beethoven

(Two-bar piano intro)

9

13. GERMAN DANCE

Mozart

(Two-bar piano intro)

14. CHORAL FANTASY

Beethoven

(Two-bar piano intro - pickup starts on beat two)

15. THE HEAVENS ARE TELLING

Haydn

(Two-bar piano intro - pickup starts on beat four)

16. BOURRÉE (Water Music)

Handel

(Two-bar piano intro - pickup starts on beat four)

17. CARNIVAL OF VENICE

Benedict

(Two-bar piano intro - pickup starts on beat three)

18. SONATINA #1

Beethoven

(Two-bar piano intro)

19. LONDONDERRY AIR

(Two-bar piano intro - pickup starts on beat two)

15

20. BLUE DANUBE

Strauss

(Two-bar piano intro - pickup starts on beat three)

21. MINUET I

Bach

(Two-bar piano intro)

22. EINE KLEINE

Mozart

(Two-bar piano intro)

23. SYMPHONY #7 (3rd Movement)

Beethoven

(Two-bar piano intro - pickup starts on beat three)

19

24. MINUET

Bach

(Two-bar piano intro)

Made in the USA
Middletown, DE
02 September 2024

60302052R00015